SandCastle
Let's Go!

LET'S GO
BY
HOVERCRAFT

ANDERS HANSON

Consulting Editor, Diane Craig, M.A./Reading Specialist

ABDO Publishing Company

Published by ABDO Publishing Company, 8000 West 78th Street, Edina, MN 55439.

Copyright © 2008 by Abdo Consulting Group, Inc. International copyrights reserved in all countries. No part of this book may be reproduced in any form without written permission from the publisher. SandCastle™ is a trademark and logo of ABDO Publishing Company.

Printed in the United States.

Editor: Pam Price
Curriculum Coordinator: Nancy Tuminelly
Cover and Interior Design and Production: Mighty Media
Photo Credits: iStockphoto (Jack Andrys, Alison Large, Jamie Myers), Shutterstock, Terry Tousignant

Library of Congress Cataloging-in-Publication Data

Hanson, Anders, 1980-

    Let's go by hovercraft / Anders Hanson.
      p. cm. -- (Let's go!)
    ISBN 978-1-59928-900-7
    1. Ground-effect machines--Juvenile literature. I. Title.

VM362.H36 2008
629.3--dc22

                                         2007014938

SandCastle™ Level: Transitional

SandCastle™ books are created by a team of professional educators, reading specialists, and content developers around five essential components—phonemic awareness, phonics, vocabulary, text comprehension, and fluency—to assist young readers as they develop reading skills and increase their general knowledge. All books are written, reviewed, and leveled for guided reading, early intervention reading, and Accelerated Reader® programs for use in shared, guided, and independent reading and writing activities to support a balanced approach to literacy instruction. The SandCastle™ series has four levels that correspond to early literacy development. The levels are provided to help teachers and parents select appropriate books for young readers.

SandCastle™	SandCastle™	SandCastle™	SandCastle™
Emerging Readers (no flags)	**Beginning Readers** (1 flag)	**Transitional Readers** (2 flags)	**Fluent Readers** (3 flags)

SandCastle™ would like to hear from you. Please send us your comments or questions.

sandcastle@abdopublishing.com

A hovercraft has
a large fan that
allows it to float
on a cushion of air.

3

A powerful fan forces air downward.

The air inflates a skirt on the bottom of the hovercraft.

Air pressure inside the skirt forces the craft upward.

A rear fan controls the craft's speed and direction.

A hovercraft can travel over land.

A hovercraft
can float above
water too.

A hovercraft
can travel over
almost any
smooth surface!

Some hovercrafts have wings. The wings let the hovercraft fly one to four feet in the air when it is going fast.

HAVE YOU EVER SEEN A HOVERCRAFT?

WHERE DID YOU SEE IT?

HOW A HOVERCRAFT FLOATS

1. A powerful fan pulls air into the hovercraft.

fan

2. The air is forced into a channel.

air channel

skirt

3. Some air exits the channel through openings near the edge.

4. Some air gets trapped inside the craft's skirt.

5. The trapped air lifts the vehicle.

Christopher Cockerell invented the hovercraft. The first one was launched in 1959.

The official world speed record for a hovercraft is 85 miles per hour.

Hoverbarges are large platforms that can transport heavy goods or equipment over most surfaces. The largest hoverbarge can remain in the air while carrying up to 330 tons.

GLOSSARY

cushion – something that provides support or protects against impact.

inflate – to fill with air or another gas.

platform – a raised flat surface.

pressure – force applied to an object.

surface – the outside layer of something.

transport – to move something from one place to another.

To see a complete list of SandCastle™ books and other nonfiction titles from ABDO Publishing Company, visit **www.abdopublishing.com**.

8000 West 78th Street, Edina, MN 55439 • 800-800-1312 • 952-831-1632 fax